Presented To

From

And now I entrust you to God and the word of His grace—His message that is able to build you up and give you an inheritance with all those He has set apart for Himself.

ACTS 20:32 NLT

A life lived in prayer
is a life never wasted.

God wants to be loved for Himself, but that is only part. He also wants us to know that when we have Him we have everything.

—A.W. TOZER

The Lord takes pleasure in His people.

PSALM 149:4 NKJV

The first thing I want you to do is pray.
Pray every way you know how,
for everyone you know.

I TIMOTHY 2:1 THE MESSAGE

The wonderful thing is,
the more we focus on Jesus,
the more clearly we see one another.

—TRIESTE VAN WYNGARDEN

A relationship with God is like
being with a person all of the time.
In Him we have a constant companion,
listener, counselor, and friend.

For we are God's masterpiece.
He has created us anew in Christ Jesus,
so we can do the good things
He planned for us long ago.

EPHESIANS 2:10 NLT

"It is written,"
He said to them,
"'My house will be called
a house of prayer.'"

MATTHEW 21:13 NIV

Try starting every day by coming up with three gifts He's given. You'll truly be entering His gates with thanksgiving, which will lead to His courts of praise. And in His presence is fullness of joy.

"When you pray fervently, you'll see things happen. Before your prayers are answered there will be blessings from God that will come to you simply because you are praying. That's because you will have spent time in the presence of God, where all lasting transformation begins."

—STORMIE OMARTIAN

He has given each one of us a special gift
through the generosity of Christ.

EPHESIANS 4:7 NLT

"As for Me, this is My covenant with them," says the Lord. "My Spirit, who is on you, and My words that I have put in your mouth will not depart from your mouth, or from the mouths of your children, or from the mouths of their descendants from this time on and forever," says the Lord.

ISAIAH 59:21 NIV

Seeking God in scripture is like pulling out the handy little tape measure on your keychain. It helps you confirm what you can only guess at otherwise.

—DEANNA RYAN

Do you put on your spiritual armor each day when you wake up? Or better yet — do you go to sleep with it on each night, and just make sure it's in place when you get out of bed in the morning? Your shield of faith is never far from your hand— and the One who strengthens it is right beside you, too.

We trust in the name of the Lord our God.

PSALM 20:7 NIV

I always thank my God as I remember you
in my prayers.

PHILEMON 1:4 NIV

Jesus' coming allowed us to approach the throne of grace with confidence. It's because of Jesus that all of God's promises are fulfilled, and we can dream the impossible for ourselves and others.

Wouldn't you love to have a hope-filled heart? Wouldn't you love to see the world through the eyes of Jesus? Where we see unanswered prayer, Jesus saw answered prayer. Where we see the absence of God, Jesus saw the plan of God... God never promises to remove us from our struggles. He does promise, however, to change the way we look at them.

—MAX LUCADO

This is what God the Lord says—
He who created the heavens
and stretched them out...
I will take hold of your hand.

ISAIAH 42:5, 6 NIV

By faith we understand that the worlds
were framed by the word of God, so that
the things which are seen were not made of
things which are visible.

HEBREWS 11:3 NKJV

God rewards those who seek Him.
Not those who seek doctrine or religion
or systems or creeds. Many settle for these
lesser passions, but the reward goes to
those who settle for nothing less than Jesus
Himself. And what is the reward?
What awaits those who seek Jesus?
Nothing short of the heart of Jesus.

—MAX LUCADO

Pray boldly, expectantly, specifically.
Your Heavenly Father loves you, so don't
be afraid to be bold in prayer.

—JOYCE MEYER

Not one of all the Lord's good promises…
failed; every one was fulfilled.

JOSHUA 21:45 NIV

If we know that He hears us—
whatever we ask—we know that we have what
we asked of Him.

I JOHN 5:15 NIV

God has a unique way of communicating
with each of us. He's designed us
to hear, see, feel, and touch Him
in a way that no one else can.
We can learn about possibilities
from other people's journeys...
but only by experiencing Him personally
can we know Him the way He intended.

To pray effectively, we must pray the answer, which is praying God's Word over the situation in order to bring God's change.

—BARBARA BILLETT

He calls His own sheep by name.

JOHN 10:3 NIV

Pray without ceasing.

1 THESSALONIANS 5:17 NIV

Going through a waiting period doesn't mean that there is nothing happening, because when you are waiting on the Lord, He is always moving in your life.

—STORMIE OMARTIAN

What does a constant conversation with God look like? It's a little like having Him on speaker phone in your heart. Neither of you ever hangs up.

I will praise You,
for I am fearfully and wonderfully made.

PSALM 139:14 NKJV

The end of all things is near.
Therefore be clear minded and self-
controlled so that you can pray.

1 PETER 4:7 NIV

The best advice is always from the Holy Spirit. Sometimes He speaks through other people, but learning to recognize His voice in all forms is an art that leads to wisdom.

Prayer is not only asking,
but is an attitude of the mind which
produces the atmosphere in which
asking is perfectly natural.

—OSWALD CHAMBERS

And the peace of God, which surpasses all understanding, will guard your hearts and minds through Christ Jesus.

PHILIPPIANS 4:7 NKJV

How much more will your Father
who is in heaven give good things
to those who ask Him!

MATTHEW 7:11 NIV

We never need to be without hope—for as we look into the future with the eyes of faith, we will see that God is already there.

—ROY LESSIN

If we have not because we ask not —
what would you ask Him for today?

I pray that you may prosper in all things
and be in health.

III JOHN 1:2 NKJV

If you live in Me
(abide vitally united to Me)
and My words remain in you and continue
to live in your hearts, ask whatever you will,
and it shall be done for you.

JOHN 15:7 AMP

If we truly understood the power of God at
work within us, and what He can
and will accomplish through us,
we would live fearlessly.
Is that possible?
Yes, it is!
It's His promise.

When I am in a moment of deep prayer,
feeling close to God and in tune with His
Spirit, I find myself nodding a lot.
"Yes, Lord, yes!" We know He can be
trusted because what He promises
becomes reality.

—LIZ CURTIS HIGGS

"He who believes in Me,"
as the Scripture has said,
"out of his heart will flow rivers
of living water."

JOHN 7:38 NKJV

When life is heavy and hard to take,
go off by yourself. Enter the silence.
Bow in prayer. Don't ask questions:
Wait for hope to appear.

LAMENTATIONS 3:28-29 THE MESSAGE

God's Son is born into me through the direct act of God; then I as His child must exercise the right of a child—the right of always being face to face with my Father through prayer. Whatever our circumstances may be, that holy, innocent, and eternal Child must be in contact with His Father.

—OSWALD CHAMBERS

What does it mean to "be still and know" who God is? It is to quietly trust, to patiently wait, to actively know, to confidently act on the faith that He is the answer to every promise—even when the answer isn't clear.

—TRIESTE VAN WYNGARDEN

He who calls you is faithful,
who also will do it.

1 THESSALONIANS 5:24 NKJV

But you, dear friends, build yourselves up in your most holy faith and pray in the Holy Spirit. Keep yourselves in God's love as you wait for the mercy of our Lord Jesus Christ to bring you to eternal life.

JUDE 1:20–21 NIV

Our best relationships on earth are poor reflections of what our friendship with God can be. No one knows us better, loves us more, or wants greater things for us than He does.

Prayer takes us to the throne of God
and we can be sure that the heart of our
King is always listening with love.

—HOLLEY GERTH

I will be your God
throughout your lifetime…
I made you, and I will care for you.

ISAIAH 46:4 NLT

If we see a Christian believer sinning...
we ask for God's help and He gladly gives
it, gives life to the sinner whose sin is not
fatal. There is such a thing as a fatal sin,
and I'm not urging you to pray about that.

I JOHN 5:16 THE MESSAGE

Faith is to see what we do not see,
and the reward of this faith
is to see what we believe.

—ST. AUGUSTINE

Instead of talking to God
about your problems,
try talking to your problems
about God.

He guides me along right paths,
bringing honor to His name.

PSALM 23:3 NLT

The grass withers and the flowers fall,
but the word of our God stands forever.

ISAIAH 40:8 NIV

With a Shepherd ready to lead us through any situation, a simple step forward is the right direction.

In prayer, it's never the size of the mountain that matters, but the strength of the mountain Mover.

—MATT ANDERSON

When dreams come true,
there is life and joy.

PROVERBS 13:12 NLT

Be anxious for nothing, but in everything by prayer and supplication, with thanksgiving, let your requests be made known to God.

PHILIPPIANS 4:6 NKJV

God's help is near and always available.

—MAX LUCADO

The chances are 100% that God is enough.

The Lord your God…has chosen you to be
His own special treasure.

DEUTERONOMY 14:2 NLT

Prayer is essential in this ongoing warfare.
Pray hard and long. Pray for your brothers
and sisters. Keep your eyes open.
Keep each other's spirits up so that no one
falls behind or drops out.

EPHESIANS 6:18 THE MESSAGE

Time in God's presence is restorative,
faith-building, and full of life.
Why would we want to be anywhere else?

Praying for others is one of the greatest gifts we can give.

—LINN CARLSON

This is the day the Lord has made.
We will rejoice and be glad in it.

PSALM 118:24 NLT

Be joyful in hope, patient in affliction,
faithful in prayer.

ROMANS 12:12 NIV

An infinite God can give all of Himself to each of His children. He does not distribute Himself that each may have a part, but to each one He gives all of Himself as full as if there were no others.

—A. W. TOZER

One of the greatest things about gratitude
is that when you thank God by faith,
you begin to really discover what you've
thanked Him for.

Be sure of this:
I am with you always,
even to the end of the age.

MATTHEW 28:20 NLT

Watch therefore, and pray always that you may be counted worthy to escape all these things that will come to pass, and to stand before the Son of Man.

LUKE 21:36 NKJV

Giving thanks
is like gaining an audience with the King;
praising Him
is like being welcomed into His home
as His beloved children.

There is nothing more powerful
than a faith-filled prayer—
it has the grace to comfort the soul
and the strength to move a mountain.

—BONNIE JENSEN

I pray that you will begin to understand the incredible greatness of His power for us who believe Him. This is the same mighty power that raised Christ from the dead and seated Him in the place of honor at God's right hand in the heavenly realms.

EPHESIANS 1:19, 20 NLT

Then Jesus told His disciples a parable
to show them that they should always pray
and not give up.

LUKE 18:1 NIV

We are either in the process of resisting God's truth or in the process of being shaped and molded by His truth.

—CHARLES STANLEY

In a constant conversation,
it's important to listen as well as to speak.
What is the still, small voice of God
speaking to your heart today?

The Lord's unfailing love surrounds the
man who trusts in Him.

PSALM 32:10 NIV

Therefore I say to you,
whatever things you ask when you pray,
believe that you receive them,
and you will have them.

MARK 11:24 NKJV

True value is found in the life of a person whose faith is looking upward, whose steps are pressing onward, and whose heart is reaching outward with Christ's love.

Three things I pray for my children—
a joyful home, a servant's heart,
and a life sold out for Jesus.

—KRISTEN STRONG

The Lord will be your everlasting light,
and your God will be your glory.

ISAIAH 60:19 NIV

Then Jeremiah the prophet said to them, "I have heard. Indeed, I will pray to the Lord your God according to your words, and it shall be, that whatever the Lord answers you, I will declare it to you. I will keep nothing back from you."

JEREMIAH 42:4 NKJV

I used to ask God to help me.
Then I asked if I might help Him.
I ended up asking God
to do His work through me.

—HUDSON TAYLOR

To breathe,
and accept that breath as life and gift,
is to praise the One who gives it.

He will not let your foot slip—He who
watches over you will not slumber.

PSALM 121:3 NIV

Make this your common practice:
Confess your sins to each other and
pray for each other so that you can live
together whole and healed. The prayer of a
person living right with God is something
powerful to be reckoned with.

JAMES 5:16 THE MESSAGE

Because of God,
we can always look ahead with hope.

Any area that doesn't have an expectation of good is under the influence of a lie.

—BILL JOHNSON

The fruit of righteousness will be peace;
the effect of righteousness will be quietness
and confidence forever.

ISAIAH 32:17 NIV

The Lord is near to all who call on Him,
to all who call on Him in truth.

PSALM 145:18 NIV

His call is to be His friend
to accomplish His purpose.

—OSWALD CHAMBERS

Being intentional about prayer time is important—like going on a date with your spouse. But it's not the only connection, it's just the special time you choose to bring focus to your relationship in the midst of doing life together on a daily basis.

Freely you have received, freely give.

MATTHEW 10:8 NIV

But if…you seek the Lord your God,
you will find Him if you look for Him with
all your heart and with all your soul.

DEUTERONOMY 4:29 NIV

In the great symphony of life,
the final refrain is triumphant,
everlasting joy for those who believe.

There is no way to learn to pray
but by praying.

—SAMUEL CHADWICK

Follow the way of love.

1 CORINTHIANS 14:1 NIV

I wait for the Lord, my soul waits,
and in His word I do hope.

PSALM 130:5 NKJV

When we pray according to the will of God,
we can be certain that God's answers are
the right answers, done in the right way,
at the right time, and for the right reason.

—ROY LESSIN

God, Help me to hear Your voice
whispering to my heart, to see Your hand
in the beauty of the world You made,
to feel Your love in the warmth of a hug.
Thank You that You speak to me
in so many ways.

I am with you...
I am your God.
I will strengthen you,
Yes, I will help you,
I will uphold you
with My righteous right hand.

ISAIAH 41:10 NKJV

Gabriel...said to me...I have now come to
give you insight and understanding.
As soon as you began to pray, an answer
was given, which I have come to tell you,
for you are highly esteemed.

DANIEL 9:21, 22, 23 NIV

It's when we most need His strength
that we realize how wonderful it is
to have Him near.

Don't pray when you feel like it. Have an appointment with the Lord and keep it. A man is powerful on his knees.

—CORRIE TEN BOOM

You shall rejoice in every good thing which
the Lord your God has given to you
and your house.

DEUTERONOMY 26:11 NKJV

"For I know the plans I have for you,"
declares the Lord, "plans to prosper you
and not to harm you, plans to give you
hope and a future. Then you will call upon
Me and come and pray to Me,
and I will listen to you."

JEREMIAH 29:11-12 NIV

God's never taken His eye off of you.
Not for a millisecond. He's always near.
He lives to hear your heartbeat.
He loves to hear your prayers.

—MAX LUCADO

Whether or not you believe in God,
He believes in you.

A good man out of the good treasure
of his heart
brings forth good.

LUKE 6:45 NKJV

Pray especially for rulers and their governments to rule well so we can be quietly about our business of living simply, in humble contemplation.

I TIMOTHY 2:2 THE MESSAGE

When the day begins to feel a little off-balance, find your center in the One who leads us through any valley or over any mountain. If you need a lift, let Him carry you for a while.

Glory to God! God is faithful
to watch over His Word to perform it.

—BARBARA BILLETT

Show me Your ways, O Lord; Teach me
Your paths. Lead me in Your truth.

PSALM 25:4 NKJV

And He who searches our hearts
knows the mind of the Spirit,
because the Spirit intercedes for the saints
in accordance with God's will.

ROMANS 8:27 NIV

If we never speak to our spouse or never listen to anything our spouse might have to say to us, our marriage relationship will quickly deteriorate. It is the same way with God. Prayer—communicating with God—helps us grow closer and more intimately connected with God.

—MARY FAIRCHILD

It's important for us to remember
that waiting times are never wasted times
when the One we are waiting on is God.

I am leaving you with a gift—
peace of mind and heart.
And the peace I give
is a gift the world cannot give.
So don't be troubled or afraid.

JOHN 14:27 NLT

Pray for the peace of Jerusalem:
"May those who love you be secure.
May there be peace within your walls and
security within your citadels." For the sake
of my brothers and friends, I will say,
"Peace be within you." For the sake of the
house of the Lord our God, I will seek
your prosperity.

PSALM 122:6–9 NIV

The best way to end the day
is to thank the One who gave it,
and all He put in it for you to enjoy.

The Christian life is not a constant high. I have my moments of deep discouragement. I have to go to God in prayer with tears in my eyes, and say, "O God, forgive me," or "Help me."

—BILLY GRAHAM

Surely your goodness and unfailing love
will pursue me all the days of my life.

PSALM 23:6 NLT

Then the Lord said to him,
"Take off your sandals;
the place where you are standing
is holy ground."

ACTS 7:33 NIV

Prayer is not asking.
Prayer is putting oneself in the hands of
God, at His disposition, and listening to
His voice in the depth of our hearts.

—MOTHER TERESA

Pray every day. Pray every moment.
Pray to listen and hear, to ask and receive,
to praise and worship, to connect and
discover, to survive and thrive.
Just pray.

For surely, O Lord,
You bless the righteous;
You surround them with Your favor.

PSALM 5:12 NIV

Likewise the Spirit also helps in our weaknesses. For we do not know what we should pray for as we ought, but the Spirit Himself makes intercession for us with groanings which cannot be uttered.

ROMANS 8:26 NKJV

The best way to start the day is to acknowledge the One who made it.

To be a Christian without prayer
is no more possible than to be alive
without breathing.

—MARTIN LUTHER

By wisdom a house is built, and through understanding it is established; through knowledge its rooms are filled with rare and beautiful treasures.

PROVERBS 24:3, 4 NIV

I am praying that you will put into action
the generosity that comes from your faith
as you understand and experience all the
good things we have in Christ.

PHILEMON 1:6 NLT

You may pray for an hour
and still not pray.
You may meet God for a moment
and then be in touch with Him all day.

—FREDRIK WISLOFF

God, I praise You for who You are.
Thank You that You are so much greater
than I am. Help me to love You more
deeply and see You more fully as I worship
You with my words and with my life.

Blessed is the man who trusts in the Lord,
whose confidence is in Him.

JEREMIAH 17:7 NIV

Since prayer is at the bottom of all this,
what I want mostly is for men to pray—
not shaking angry fists at enemies but
raising holy hands to God.

I TIMOTHY 2:8 THE MESSAGE

Faith doesn't occupy itself with outward things; it is an act of the will...an inward choice that says, "I don't see, but I believe. I can't understand, but I trust."

Prayer does not change God,
but it changes him who prays.

—SØREN KIERKEGAARD

He will be an instrument for noble purposes, made holy, useful to the Master and prepared to do any good work.

II TIMOTHY 2:21 NIV

I will pray morning, noon, and night…
and He will hear and answer.

PSALM 55:17 TLB

One of the most arduous spiritual tasks is that of giving up control and allowing the Spirit of God to lead our lives.

—HENRI NOUWEN

Lord, this is a good day!
I might not know enough about it yet to say
WHY it's a good day—
but I trust You who made it to lead the way.
I will rejoice and be glad in You and all
You have in store.

Yours, O Lord, is the kingdom; You are exalted as head over all. Wealth and honor come from You; You are the ruler of all things. In Your hands are strength and power to exalt and give strength to all.

I CHRONICLES 29:11, 12 NIV

Praise the Lord…
for He loves us very dearly.

PSALM 117:1, 2 TLB

The true expression of Christian character is not in good-doing, but in God-likeness. If the Spirit of God has transformed you within, you will exhibit divine characteristics in your life, not just good human characteristics.

—OSWALD CHAMBERS

Any concern too small
to be turned into a prayer
is too small to be made into a burden.

—CORRIE TEN BOOM

Where can I go from your Spirit?
Where can I flee from Your presence?
If I go up to the heavens, You are there;
if I make my bed in the depth, You are
there. If I rise on the wings of the dawn,
if I settle on the far side of the sea, even
there Your hand will guide me.
Your right hand will hold me fast.

PSALM 139:7–10 NIV

Ask, and it will be given to you;
seek, and you will find; knock,
and it will be opened to you.

MATTHEW 7:7 NKJV

I love to think of nature
as an unlimited broadcasting station,
through which God speaks to us every
hour, if we will only tune in.

—GEORGE WASHINGTON CARVER

In God's presence is fullness of joy—
enough of everything we need,
and so much more.

For this reason I kneel before the Father,
from whom His whole family in heaven
and on earth derives its name.

EPHESIANS 3:14, 15 NIV

The heavens declare the glory of God;
the skies proclaim the work of His hands.

PSALM 19:1 NIV

Faith shines even brighter
when the road ahead looks dark.

Prayer is nothing else than being on terms
of friendship with God.

—SAINT TERESA OF AVILA

Everyone who asks receives;
he who seeks finds;
and to him who knocks,
the door will be opened.

MATTHEW 7:8 NIV

I can never stop thanking God for all the wonderful gifts He's given.

I CORINTHIANS 1:4 TLB

Trusting is an act of worship.
Just as parents are pleased when children
trust their love and wisdom,
your faith makes God happy.

—RICK WARREN

He never condemns.
He never shames.
He always knows,
always validates.
Sometimes disciplines...
but always loves.

We have access by faith
into this grace in which we stand,
and rejoice in hope of the glory of God.

ROMANS 5:2 NKJV

This is the confidence we have in
approaching God: that if we ask anything
according to His will, He hears us.

I JOHN 5:14 NIV

In order to respond to the blessings God has given us, faith doesn't need a complicated formula, it only needs a simple truth spoken by a faithful God.

How great is the prayer,
how rich is the meaning, how full is the
gratefulness of those who can say,
"I thank God for you."

—ROY LESSIN

OCTOBER 10

May Your unfailing love rest upon us,
O Lord, even as we put our hope in You.

PSALM 33:22 NIV

I will praise You, O Lord my God,
with all my heart.

PSALM 86:12 NIV

It is love that asks,
that seeks, that knocks,
that finds, and that is faithful
to what it finds.

—ST. AUGUSTINE

Our best, most fulfilling relationships on
earth are just the tiniest glimpse
of the intimacy, friendship,
and love we can know with God.

He will be their peace.

MICAH 5:5 NIV

How grateful I am to the Lord
because He is so good.

PSALM 7:17 TLB

Faith is the common thread that binds our hearts together in Christ's love.

It is a common temptation of Satan to
make us give up the reading of the Word
and prayer when our enjoyment is gone;
as if it were of no use to read the Scriptures
when we do not enjoy them,
and as if it were no use to pray when we
have no spirit of prayer.

—GEORGE MULLER

He who did not spare His own Son,
but gave Him up for us all—
how will He not also, along with Him,
graciously give us all things?

ROMANS 8:32 NIV

As far as the east is from the west,
so far has He removed
our transgressions from us.

PSALM 103:11 NIV

Learn to worship God
as the God who does wonders,
who wishes to prove in you that He can do
something supernatural and divine.

—ANDREW MURRAY

Prayer is aligning oneself
with the purposes of God.

—E. STANLEY JONES

Live a life of love, just as Christ loved us and gave Himself up for us as a fragrant offering and sacrifice to God.

EPHESIANS 5:2 NIV

God who began the good work within you
will keep right on helping you grow.

PHILIPPIANS 1:6 TLB

God's love is endless... faithful...
and pure... and to Him,
you are a priceless treasure.

To acknowledge Him in the most normal
of moments, to turn your attention to Him
in silent thanks for the everyday—
that alone is worship.

He is the one who invited you into this wonderful friendship with His Son, Jesus Christ our Lord.

1 CORINTHIANS 1:9 NLT

Bless God and sing His praises;
for He holds our lives in His hands.

PSALM 66:8, 9 TLB

Prayer is the exercise
of drawing on the grace of God.

—OSWALD CHAMBERS

A sacrifice of praise
quickly becomes the gift of worship.

So let us come boldly to the throne of our gracious God. There we will receive His mercy, and we will find grace to help us when we need it.

HEBREWS 4:16 NLT

Listen to His voice, and hold fast to Him.
For the Lord is your life.

DEUTERONOMY 30:20 NIV

He is the greatest One to know;
the wisest One to follow;
the perfect One to trust;
the faithful One to serve;
the highest One to love.

God,
You have blessed me so much, and I want
to share my gratitude with You.
Thank You so much for who You are,
for Your amazing love in my life, and for
all the ways You are so good to me!

No eye has seen, no ear has heard,
and no mind has imagined what God has
prepared for those who love Him.

I CORINTHIANS 2:9 NLT

Think about all you can praise God for
and be glad about.

PHILIPPIANS 4:8 TLB

To get nations back on their feet,
we must first get down on our knees.

—BILLY GRAHAM

Don't let the enemy push you into a battle
you are not ready for.
Keep your focus on Jesus, and natural
obstacles will arise because of that.

—GRAHAM COOKE

I am the Lord, the God...
Is anything too hard for Me?

JEREMIAH 32:27 NLT

I lay my requests before You
and wait in expectation.

PSALM 5:3 NIV

In prayer, we have a place
where faith flows freely
and hope runs deep;
a place where we can go
to be refreshed
and to remember who we really are.

When Jesus calls us blessed, He is explaining the life we live when the Holy Spirit has His unhindered way with us. Blessed are those who receive!

Then joy will accompany him in his work all the days of the life God has given him.

ECCLESIASTES 8:15 NIV

Lord, with all my heart I thank You.

PSALM 138:1 TLB

It is possible to move men,
through God, by prayer alone.

—HUDSON TAYLOR

As you keep praying,
God will keep working.

—JOYCE MEYER

The fruit of the Spirit is love, joy, peace, patience, kindness, goodness, faithfulness.

GALATIANS 5:22 NIV

For You are indeed God,
and Your words are truth.

II SAMUEL 7:28 TLB

There is great joy in asking the Lord
for the things He wants for us.
It's a perfect partnership.

Trusting God has never turned out poorly.

You will find your joy in the Lord.

ISAIAH 58:14 NIV

Thank you, Lord! How good You are!
Your love for us continues forever.

PSALM 106:1 TLB

God shapes the world by prayer.
The more praying there is in the world the
better the world will be, the mightier the
forces against evil.

—E. M. BOUNDS

The power of prayer is in the One who hears it and not the one who says it. Our prayers do make a difference.

—MAX LUCADO

The things You planned for us
no one can recount to You.

PSALM 40:5 NIV

The widow who is really in need
and left all alone puts her hope in God
and continues night and day to pray
and to ask God for help.

I TIMOTHY 5:5 NIV

God doesn't call the qualified…
He qualifies the called.
If you say yes to Him,
He'll say yes to you!

How do you spell faith? R-I-S-K.
How will you live out your faith today?
What boldness will you ask Him for?

May He work in us what is pleasing to
Him, through Jesus Christ,
to whom be glory for ever and ever.

HEBREWS 13:21 NIV

The next day, as they went on their journey
and drew near the city, Peter went up on
the housetop to pray, about the sixth hour.

ACTS 10:9 NKJV

In worship, God imparts Himself to us.

—C. S. LEWIS

Prayer is simply a two-way conversation
between you and God.

—BILLY GRAHAM

Those who know Your name
will trust in You, for You, Lord,
have never forsaken those who seek You.

PSALM 9:10 NIV

If we confess our sins to Him,
He can be depended on to forgive us.

I JOHN 1:9 TLB

Prayer can move mountains,
while human effort can move a pile of dirt
from one spot to another.

Talking to God isn't a phone call.
It's a road trip with your best friend.

Praise be to the Lord,
to God our Savior,
who daily bears our burdens.

PSALM 68:19 NIV

But when you pray, go into your room, close the door and pray to your Father, who is unseen. Then your Father, who sees what is done in secret, will reward you.

MATTHEW 6:6 NIV

Nothing tends more to cement the hearts of Christians than praying together. Never do they love one another so well as when they witness the outpouring of each other's hearts in prayer.

—CHARLES FINNEY

Prayer is not monologue, but dialogue.
God's voice in response to mine
is its most essential part.

—ANDREW MURRAY

It is good to give thanks to the Lord,
and to sing praises to Your name,
O Most High; to declare Your
lovingkindness in the morning,
and Your faithfulness every night.

PSALM 92:1–2 NKJV

If You, O Lord, kept a record of sins...
who could stand?
But with You there is forgiveness.

PSALM 130:3, 4 NIV

There are few things as meaningful as agreeing with someone else in prayer. It brings a contentment and peace like no other experience.

If God's kindness is what brings us to repentance, then we can be sure any voice of harsh condemnation is not His voice.

Truly our fellowship is with the Father and
with His Son Jesus Christ.

1 JOHN 1:3 NKJV

Love one another deeply,
from the heart.

I PETER 1:22 NIV

There is not in the world a kind of life more sweet and delightful that that of a continual conversation with God.

—BROTHER LAWRENCE

The sound of "gentle stillness" after all the thunder and wind have passed will be the ultimate Word from God.

—JIM ELLIOT

Trust in Him at all times, you people;
pour out your heart before Him;
God is a refuge for us.

PSALM 62:8 NKJV

Pray diligently. Stay alert,
with your eyes wide open in gratitude.

COLOSSIANS 4:2 THE MESSAGE

A successful day is one in which you've connected with the Father, followed the Son, and listened to the Holy Spirit.

Thanksgiving is the welcome mat,
praise is the doorway,
and God's presence
is the comfortable home
we keep with Him.

I've listened to your prayer and I've
observed your tears. I'm going to heal you.

II KINGS 20:5 THE MESSAGE

I pray for them. I'm not praying for the God-rejecting world But for those You gave Me, For they are Yours by right.

JOHN 17:9 THE MESSAGE

There is a mighty lot of difference between saying prayers and praying.

—JOHN G. LAKE

Prayer in the sense of petition, asking for things, is a small part of it; confession and penitence are its threshold, adoration its sanctuary, the presence and vision and enjoyment of God its bread and wine.

—C.S. LEWIS

Now let Your unfailing love comfort me,
just as You promised me, Your servant.

PSALM 119:76 NLT

We love because He first loved us.

I JOHN 4:19 NIV

Prayer isn't about what we can accomplish
with God's help. It's about who we can be
by His hand.

Anything that is asked of us, is first given.
Do you need to show someone mercy?
Come to Him with a humble heart and
allow His mercy to be poured out on you.

Guide me in Your truth and teach me,
for You are God my Savior,
and my hope is in You all day long.

PSALM 25:5 NIV

And now these three remain: faith, hope, and love. But the greatest of these is love.

I CORINTHIANS 13:13 NIV

The point of prayer is not to get answers
from God, but to have perfect and
complete oneness with Him.
When you seem to have no answer, there
is always a reason—God uses these times to
give you deep personal instruction, and it
is not for anyone else but you.

—OSWALD CHAMBERS

I live in the spirit of prayer. I pray as I walk
and when I lie down and when I arise.
And the answers are always coming.

—GEORGE MULLER

I always pray for you, and I make my requests with a heart full of joy.

PHILIPPIANS 1:4 NLT

What makes you think God won't step in
and work justice for His chosen people,
who continue to cry out for help?
Won't he stick up for them? I assure you,
He will. He will not drag His feet.

LUKE 18:7-8 THE MESSAGE

God will often place desires in our hearts, just so He can fulfill them. Listen to your longings, and ask the Lord if they're specially placed in your heart by Him.

God,
Thank You that You know every need I
have before I even bring it to You.
Thank You that You know
the needs of those I love too.
As I bring my requests before You,
I trust that You are able to answer in ways
even greater than I can imagine.

He fills my life with good things.

PSALM 103:5 NLT

You will seek Me and find me when you
seek Me with all your heart.

JEREMIAH 29:13 NIV

To pray in Jesus' name means to pray in
His spirit, in His compassion, in His love,
in His outrage, in His concern.
In other words, it means to pray a prayer
that Jesus Himself might pray.

—KENNETH L. WILSON

I wait on God to bring to pass
all He has promised me,
and as I wait, I rest in faith
in what I cannot see.
For in His way He will provide
at just the perfect time
everything that's good and right
to bless this life of mine.

—ROY LESSIN

The Lord is God, and He created the heavens and earth and put everything in place. He made the world to be lived in, not to be a place of empty chaos. "I am the Lord," He says, "and there is no other."

ISAIAH 45:18 NLT

Then when you pray, God will answer.
You'll call out for help and I'll say,
"Here I am."

ISAIAH 58:9 THE MESSAGE

Why waste time praying for the things God
has already promised to provide?
Dream big, and you'll most certainly find
Him there waiting.

When we say "Here I am" to God, He says,
"I've been waiting! So glad you came."

Our lives are a fragrance
presented by Christ to God.

II CORINTHIANS 2:15 NLT

Let us love one another,
for love comes from God.

I JOHN 4:7 NIV

Every great movement of God
can be traced to a kneeling figure.

—D. L. MOODY

Peace does not dwell in outward things,
but in the heart prepared to wait trustfully
and quietly on Him who has all things
safely in His hands.

—ELISABETH ELLIOT

Put on the full armor of God
so that you can take your stand
against the devil's schemes.

EPHESIANS 6:11 NIV

After He had dismissed them,
He went up on a mountainside
by Himself to pray.

MATTHEW 14:23 NIV

God never leaves us in the same place;
He transforms us from glory to glory.
If you're feeling stretched, challenged, and
out on a limb, then chances are
you're right where He wants you.

It's more than okay to take time alone
to be refreshed and restored with the Lord.
It's the example set by Jesus,
and even the Creator — on the seventh day,
even He rested.

By day the Lord directs His love,
at night His song is with me—
a prayer to the God of my life.

PSALM 42:8 NIV

Take words with you and return to the Lord. Say to Him: "Forgive all our sins and receive us graciously, that we may offer the fruit of our lips."

HOSEA 14:2 NIV

The function of prayer is not to influence
God, but rather to change the nature of
the one who prays.

—SØREN KIERKEGAARD

There is no force on earth stronger or more effective than the power of praying to our all-knowing, almighty God.

—LINN CARLSON

Who is it that overcomes the world?
Only he who believes that Jesus
is the Son of God.

I JOHN 5:5 NIV

Seek God while He's here to be found,
pray to Him while He's close at hand.

ISAIAH 55:6 THE MESSAGE

If it seems like God isn't answering a prayer, make sure you're confident about what His answers look and sound like.

God wants to partner with us in His plans.
He doesn't need our help; but when we
offer, He uses our "yes" for His good.

Whoever drinks the water I give him will never thirst. Indeed, the water I give him will become in him a spring of water welling up to eternal life.

JOHN 4:14 NIV

He said to them, "When you pray, say: 'Father, hallowed be Your name, Your kingdom come. Give us each day our daily bread. Forgive us our sins, for we also forgive everyone who sins against us. And lead us not into temptation.'"

LUKE 11:2–4 NIV

Prayer is not a mysterious practice reserved only for clergy and the religiously devout. Prayer is simply communicating with God—listening and talking to him. Believers can pray from the heart, freely, spontaneously, and in their own words.

—MARY FAIRCHILD

Through prayer you can gather the riches
of Heaven and bring them down to earth…
you can delight in the beauty of Heaven
and carry it in your heart…you can enjoy
the fellowship of Heaven and walk in it
throughout the day.

—ROY LESSIN

Trust in the Lord with all your heart…in all your ways acknowledge Him, and He will make your paths straight.

PROVERBS 3:5, 6 NIV

But I tell you: Love your enemies and pray for those who persecute you, that you may be sons of your Father in heaven.
He causes His sun to rise on the evil and the good, and sends rain on the righteous and the unrighteous.

MATTHEW 5:44–45 NIV

How often do you set apart the events of
your day for the Lord's work?
Do you devote your chores, relationships,
or willingness to serve?
Do you pause before each segment of your
day and say, "Lord, you can have this—
I trust You to handle it well,
and in my best interest"?

If God is the answer, then trying to live
without Him will leave you with
a whole lot of questions.

AUGUST 11

Come to Me, all you who are weary and
burdened, and I will give you rest.

MATTHEW 11:28 NIV

Blessed is the man who does not walk in
the counsel of the wicked or stand in the
way of sinners or sit in the seat of mockers.
But his delight is in the law of the Lord,
and on His law he meditates day and night.

PSALM 1:1-2 NIV

Prayer is putting oneself in the hands of God, and listening to His voice in the depth of our hearts.

—MOTHER TERESA

If we WATCH Him, WALK with Him, WAIT on Him, WORSHIP Him, and LIVE in His word—WE WILL WIN this battle.

—STORMIE OMARTIAN

The Lord will provide.

GENESIS 22:14 NIV

In returning and rest you shall be saved;
In quietness and confidence
shall be your strength.

ISAIAH 30:15 NKJV

As we look to Jesus and get to know Him, our other relationships naturally benefit.

No day is ever made worse by pressing in.
Seek His heart, do His will, and it will all
work for the good of those who love Him,
including you.

I am the vine; you are the branches.
If a man remains in Me and I in him,
he will bear much fruit;
apart from Me you can do nothing.

JOHN 15:5 NIV

I am the bread of life. He who comes to Me
will never go hungry, and he who believes
in Me will never be thirsty...
Everyone who looks to the Son and believes
in Him shall have eternal life.

JOHN 6:35, 40 NIV

Our rest lies in looking to the Lord,
not to ourselves.

—WATCHMAN NEE

Jesus is with you…as a comfort that is sure,
as a peace that is certain,
as a hope that is secure.

—BONNIE JENSEN

If we love one another, God abides in us,
and His love has been perfected in us.

1 JOHN 4:12 NKJV

As a shepherd looks after his scattered
flock when he is with them,
so will I look after My sheep.

EZEKIEL 34:12 NIV

Isn't it amazing to think that Jesus is before the throne of God right now, standing on your behalf? Whatever we wish, when we remain in Him, He promises to do.

The greater the need, the greater the opportunity for a great big miracle.

Many waters cannot quench love;
rivers cannot wash it away.

SONG OF SOLOMON 8:7 NIV

Look to the Lord and His strength;
seek His face always.

PSALM 105:4 NIV

My prayer is that you will find some word, some verse, or some thought that will convince you that God is very near.
I pray that as you read you will be reminded that the same voice that stilled the rage on the Sea of Galilee can still the storm in your world. Be assured—
He is closer than you've ever dreamed.

—MAX LUCADO

Sometimes the Lord prefers giving us a promise instead of an answer. Promises give hope. Hope is the atmosphere that faith grows in. Embracing His process gives us the privilege of being a part of the answer.

—BILL JOHNSON

I have no greater joy than to hear that my children are walking in the truth.

III JOHN 1:4 NIV

All things are possible with God.

MARK 10:27 NIV

Praying isn't just about expressing needs…
it's about building trust in a relationship
with the Father.

Don't forget to remember God in the details of your day. He made the day; He made the details, and you weren't meant to handle them alone.

Maybe you were made...
for just such a time as this.

ESTHER 4:14 THE MESSAGE

Take a good look at God's wonders—
they'll take your breath away.

PSALM 66:5 THE MESSAGE

"Each prayer
sets something powerful in motion."

—STORMIE OMARTIAN

FAITH goes up the stairs that LOVE has made and looks out of the windows which HOPE has opened.

—CHARLES SPURGEON

"Keep alert and pray.
Otherwise temptation will overpower you.
For though the spirit is willing enough,
the body is weak!"

MATTHEW 26:41

If we know that He hears us—
whatever we ask—we know that we have what
we asked of Him.

1 JOHN 5:15 NIV

If we could accomplish things without prayer, we wouldn't need Christ in us or the Holy Spirit to guide. The need for prayer is a reminder of the need for God, and vice versa.

God,
You know I'm not perfect,
and yet You love me anyway. Thank You
for accepting me unconditionally. I ask
for Your forgiveness and help in the areas
where I'm still growing.

When you pray, don't babble on and on as people of other religions do. They think their prayers are answered only by repeating their words again and again.

MATTHEW 6:7 NLT

Counting on God's rule to prevail, I take
heart and gain strength. I run like a deer.
I feel like I'm king of the mountain!

HABAKKUK 3:19 THE MESSAGE

Prayer is powerful
because we believe in a God
who has all power.

—ROY LESSIN

Knowing that God knows our need
doesn't keep us from praying;
it allows us to pray in faith.

—ROY LESSIN

Seth also had a son,
and he named him Enosh.
At that time men began to call
on the name of the Lord.

GENESIS 4:26 NIV

The gracious hand of our God
is on everyone who looks to Him.

EZRA 8:22 NIV

The journey with God can't be rushed.
It takes a lifetime of one step after another.

How can you know someone without investing time and interest? How can you be known without opening your heart? How can you build relationship with God without meeting with Him?

That's impossible—but fortunately there's no need to go without any part.

He is always present.

Afterward they will return to the Lord their
God and to the Messiah, their King,
and they shall come trembling,
submissive to the Lord
and to His blessings.

HOSEA 3:5 TLB

I look behind me and You're there,
then up ahead and You're there, too—
Your reassuring presence, coming and
going. This is too much, too wonderful—
I can't take it all in!

PSALM 139:5, 6 THE MESSAGE

Prayer makes the impossible possible.

—MATT ANDERSON

Our Heavenly Father has promised
to take care of us. God is for us,
with us, under us,
upholding us, around us,
and watching over us.

—JOYCE MEYER

The poor will eat and be satisfied;
they who seek the Lord will praise Him—
may your hearts live forever!

PSALM 22:26 NIV

In keeping with His promise we are looking
forward to a new heaven and a new earth,
the home of righteousness.

II PETER 3:13 NIV

In Jesus we have a constant companion.
He meant what He said when he promised,
"Never will I leave you or forsake you."

The only One who knows what we can truly
accomplish when we partner with Him
is asking for our partnership.
That's a pretty good motivator!

The Lord your God is with you,
He is mighty to save.
He will take great delight in you,
He will quiet you with His love,
He will rejoice over you with singing.

ZEPHANIAH 3:17 NIV

The Lord be with you.

RUTH 2:4 NKJV

You don't have to talk God
into being good to you—
He already has a good plan laid out.

—JOYCE MEYER

The seeds of our faith,
planted in prayer, will bring forth life,
and grow into fruit that is eternal.

—STORMIE OMARTIAN

Again, I tell you that if two of you on earth agree about anything you ask for, it will be done for you by My Father in heaven.

MATTHEW 18:19 NIV

This is the confidence we have in approaching God: that if we ask anything according to His will, He hears us.

I JOHN 5:14 NIV

The ironic characteristic of spiritual strength is that it requires more dependence and leaning into Him. More trust and faith that the struggle will give birth to that which can be born no other way. Contentment in "all circumstances" comes from going "through" the circumstances, and seeing His faithfulness and love on the other side.

—DEANNA RYAN

Father,
Thank You for loving me and wanting the best for me! I want so much to have a heart aligned with Your will, so that You will hear and answer my prayers. Please search my heart and purify it to righteousness. Teach me to want what You want.

I delight greatly in the Lord;
my soul rejoices in my God.

ISAIAH 61:10 NIV

Let's take a good look at the way we're living
and reorder our lives under God.

LAMENTATIONS 3:40 THE MESSAGE

Pray about BIG THINGS...
Pray about SMALL THINGS...
Because God cares about ALL THINGS
in your life.

—ROY LESSIN

Tell God what hurts. Talk to Him. He won't turn you away. He won't think it's silly. "For our high priest is able to understand our weaknesses. When He lived on earth, He was tempted in every way that we are, but He did not sin. Let us, then, feel very sure that we can come before God's throne where there is grace."

(HEBREWS 14:15–16 NCV)

—MAX LUCADO

Praying for you and asking God to fill you with the knowledge of His will through all spiritual wisdom and understanding.

COLOSSIANS 1:9 NIV

Now to Him who is able to do
immeasurably more than all we ask or
imagine…be glory.

EPHESIANS 3:20, 21 NIV

It's really okay to tell God everything.
He knows already, so being honest with
Him will not surprise Him in the least.

The tangible nature of God in and through us makes it possible to have real conversations with Him. If you don't call your friend "thee" or "thou," God doesn't expect that of you either.

The Lord is a refuge for the oppressed,
a stronghold in times of trouble.

PSALM 9:9 NIV

For the kingdom of God
is not a matter of talk but of power.

I CORINTHIANS 4:20 NIV

It's our job to pray.
It's God's job to answer.
Trust Him to do His job.

—STORMIE OMARTIAN

God is looking for people to use, and if you can get usable, He will wear you out. The most dangerous prayer you can pray is this: "Use me."

—RICK WARREN

Pray for us. We are sure that we have a clear conscience and desire to live honorably in every way. I particularly urge you to pray so that I may be restored to you soon.

HEBREWS 13:18–19 NIV

Delight yourself in the Lord and He will
give you the desires of your heart.

PSALM 37:4 NIV

God,
Thank You for the people in my life.
Each of them are a gift from You.
I ask that You would bless them,
and help me to love them like You do.

Jesus had a habit of talking to His Father out loud. We can learn from this that God is present enough to speak AND hear. Next time you're in traffic or in a crowd, try directing your thoughts and words toward Him. He's the only One who can truly change your circumstances.

Let us fix our eyes on Jesus, the author and perfecter of our faith, who for the joy set before Him endured the cross, scorning its shame, and sat down at the right hand of the throne of God.

HEBREWS 12:2 NIV

But for you who revere My name,
the Sun of righteousness will rise with
healing in its wings.

MALACHI 4:2 NIV

Your silent prayers uttered on tearstained pillows were heard before they were said. Your deepest questions were answered before they were asked.

—MAX LUCADO

JUNE 27

How wonderful
that no one need wait a single moment
before starting to change the world.

—ANNE FRANK

Do not merely listen to the word,
and so deceive yourselves.
Do what it says.

JAMES 1:22 NIV

The Lord longs to be gracious to you;
He rises to show you compassion.

ISAIAH 30:18 NIV

There's never a time, a situation,
a moment, when listening for the voice of
the Lord is a poor choice. He is constantly
singing over you, encouraging you, and
leading you toward His loving presence.

The Source of all wisdom and knowledge
longs to know you better,
and to tell you what He knows.

The Lord looks down from heaven on the sons of men to see if there are any who understand, any who seek God.

PSALM 14:2 NIV

One way that we can make a difference
in people's lives is to pray for them.

—ROY LESSIN

He will be the sure foundation for your times, a rich store of salvation and wisdom and knowledge; the fear of the Lord is the key to this treasure.

ISAIAH 33:6